Write It Right

Writing a News Article

By Cecilia Minden and Kate Roth

Published in the United States of America by
Cherry Lake Publishing
Ann Arbor, Michigan
www.cherrylakepublishing.com

Reading Adviser: Marla Conn MS, Ed., Literacy specialist, Read-Ability, Inc.
Book Designer: Felicia Macheske
Character Illustrator: Carol Herring

Photo Credits: © Dasha Rosato/Shutterstock, 5; © wavebreakmedia/Shutterstock.com, 7, 13; © Zurijeta/Shutterstock, 11; © akachai studio/Shutterstock, 17; © Kristoff Meller/Shutterstock, 19;

Graphics Throughout: © simple surface/Shutterstock.com; © Mix3r/Shutterstock.com; © Artefficient/Shutterstock.com; © lemony/Shutterstock.com; © Svetolk/Shutterstock.com; © EV-DA/Shutterstock.com; © briddy/Shutterstock.com; © IreneArt/Shutterstock.com

Copyright © 2020 by Cherry Lake Publishing
All rights reserved. No part of this book may be reproduced or utilized in any form or by any means without written permission from the publisher.

Library of Congress Cataloging-in-Publication Data

Names: Minden, Cecilia, author. | Roth, Kate, author. | Herring, Carol, illustrator.
Title: Writing a news article / by Cecilia Minden and Kate Roth ; illustrated by Carol Herring.
Description: Ann Arbor : Cherry Lake Publishing, [2019] | Series: Write it right | Includes bibliographical references and index.
Identifiers: LCCN 2019006005| ISBN 9781534147225 (hardcover) | ISBN 9781534148659 (pdf) | ISBN 9781534150089 (pbk.) | ISBN 9781534151512 (hosted ebook)
Subjects: LCSH: Journalism—Authorship—Juvenile literature. | Report writing—Juvenile literature.
Classification: LCC PN4776 .M55 2019 | DDC 070—dc23
LC record available at https://lccn.loc.gov/2019006005

Cherry Lake Publishing would like to acknowledge the work of The Partnership for 21st Century Skills. Please visit *www.p21.org* for more information.

Printed in the United States of America
Corporate Graphics

Table of Contents

CHAPTER ONE
Read All About It! 4

CHAPTER TWO
Get the Facts 8

CHAPTER THREE
Building Your Article 10

CHAPTER FOUR
Here's the Story 14

CHAPTER FIVE
Making Headlines 16

CHAPTER SIX
Your Own Byline 20

GLOSSARY 22
FOR MORE INFORMATION 23
INDEX 24
ABOUT THE AUTHORS 24

CHAPTER ONE

Read All About It!

We can learn new things by reading news **articles**. News articles can tell us about events in our school or town. They can also tell us about events far away. Articles may be about events that just happened. They might be about events that are about to happen.

News articles give us details and facts that we might not have known. People who write these articles are called **reporters**. Let's give reporting a try!

Newspapers are a good source to learn about events.

Write about what is happening in your town.

News articles must be **current**. They should be of interest to many readers. "Jim took a spelling test" isn't news. "Every third grader in the city scored 100 on spelling tests for 10 weeks in a row" is news. This would be of interest to many people. That's what makes it news.

Reporters are good listeners. They come up with ideas for articles by listening to what people are saying. Are most of your friends talking about the same thing? Chances are it would make a good news story.

The internet is another place where you can find trending topics.

ACTIVITY

Choose Your Story

HERE'S WHAT YOU'LL NEED:
- Pencil
- Paper

INSTRUCTIONS:
1. Think about current events at your school or in your town.
2. Think about topics all your friends are talking about.
3. Make a list of ideas for your news article.
4. Choose one to write about.

WHAT ARE PEOPLE TALKING ABOUT?
- New class president ✓
- Library book sale
- School musical
- Band bake sale

CHAPTER TWO

Get the Facts

Reporters do research to get the facts for their articles. They talk to people. They ask *who, what, where, when, why,* and *how* questions. They write down the answers to those questions.

Make sure your news articles contain facts. Two people or groups might not agree about the facts. Be sure to talk to both sides. That way, readers can make an informed choice about the topic. Use at least two **sources** of information to **verify** the facts you gather.

Be a responsible reporter and double-check your facts.

ACTIVITY

Gather Information

In this activity, you will do research to get the facts for your article.

INSTRUCTIONS:

1. Do research to find facts that answer these questions: who, what, where, when, why, and how.
2. Talk to people who were involved in the event. Write down exactly what they say.
3. Ask an adult to help you find current information online.

WHO? Candidates include: Ethan, Olivia, Zayden, and Mia
WHAT? Election for class president
WHERE? Our school
WHEN? First Monday in October
WHY? The person elected last spring moved away
HOW? How did the school run the special election?
- Students from each homeroom presented a **platform** to their class.
- One student from each homeroom was elected to run.
- Mia Alvaros was elected class president.

CHAPTER THREE

Building Your Article

Next you need to think about how to organize your article. News articles begin with a **lead**. The lead is an opening sentence that gets your readers' attention. Follow your lead with two or three paragraphs about what happened. This is the **body** of your article. Finally, write the **conclusion**. This is how the story ends.

Here is how one well-known nursery rhyme might work as a news article:

Jack and Jill went up the hill ← THE LEAD
To fetch a pail of water
Jack fell down and broke his crown ← THE BODY
And Jill came tumbling after ← THE CONCLUSION

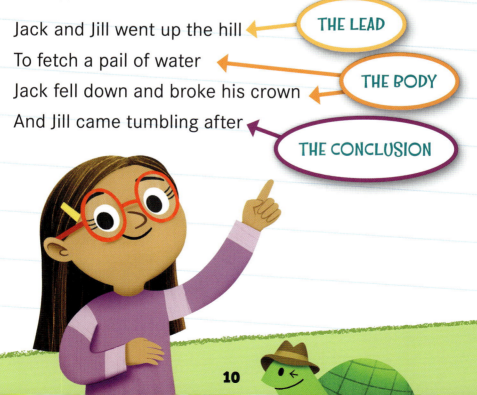

Make a rough outline of your ideas before you begin.

ACTIVITY

Organize Your Article

In this activity, you will organize the information you have gathered.

INSTRUCTIONS:

1. Organize your research into the different parts of your news article. You'll have a lead, the body paragraphs, and a conclusion.
2. Write a lead sentence to get your readers' attention.
3. List the facts that will go in each paragraph.
4. Plan your conclusion.

LEAD: Mia Alvaros was elected class president in a new election last Monday afternoon.

FACTS for Paragraph #1:
- Mia Alvaros was elected class president.
- The previous class president moved to another state.
- There was a new election for another class president.

FACTS for Paragraph #2:
- Each homeroom held an election.
- Students presented their platform to their class.
- Each homeroom elected a candidate.
- The four candidates had a new election on Monday.

CONCLUSION: Mia Alvaros won the election and is the new class president.

Staying organized helps you know where your story is going.

CHAPTER FOUR

Here's the Story

Your goal as a reporter is to interest your readers. You do this by writing in an **engaging** way. A news article should be more than a list of facts. Don't just tell what happened. Try to tell the story using the words of people you interviewed.

ACTIVITY

Write the News Article

In this activity, you will write your article in an engaging way.

INSTRUCTIONS:

1. Use the plan you created in the previous activity as a guide.
2. Write a lead sentence to get your readers' attention.
3. Write each paragraph. Use the facts in your plan to write at least three sentences for each paragraph.
4. Make your writing engaging. Include exactly what people said. Try to include fun facts.
5. Write your conclusion.

News Article Draft

Mia Alvaros was elected class president last Monday afternoon. "I'm so excited and honored to have the support of my fellow students," said Alvaros.

Raj Bansal was elected class president last spring, but his family moved to New York in August. A new election was needed to fill the post.

Each homeroom elected a candidate to run for president. Four names, one from each homeroom, went on the final ballot: Ethan Knox, Mia Alvaros, Olivia Snow, and Zayden Jackson.

On Monday, each class member had a chance to vote for their choice. It was a close race, but the final tally showed a clear winner.

Mia Alvaros has been a student here since kindergarten. She has participated in many school activities, including track, choir, and book club. Alvaros promised to work for all students and to make this the best year ever.

CHAPTER FIVE

Making Headlines

A catchy **headline** will get readers' attention. A headline is the title of your news article. A headline tells a story in just a few words. It helps readers decide whether or not to read your story.

You may want to add a picture to your story. A picture can help draw in readers. A **caption** usually appears under the picture.

A caption is one or two sentences that describe what is happening in the picture. Include the names of any people in the picture.

ACTIVITY

Add a Headline and Pictures

In this activity, you will write a headline and **illustrate** your article.

HERE'S WHAT YOU'LL NEED:

- Pencil
- Crayons or colored pencils
- A photograph of the event

INSTRUCTIONS:

1. Write a headline for your news article.
2. Choose a photograph of the event or draw a picture
3. Are there people in your photograph? If so, ask their permission to be included.
4. Write a caption for your picture.

A photo will catch the eye of the reader.

News Article

ALVAROS ELECTED CLASS PRESIDENT

Mia Alvaros was elected class president last Monday afternoon. "I'm so excited and honored to have the support of my fellow students," said Alvaros.

Raj Bansal was elected class president last spring, but his family moved to New York in August. A new election was needed to fill the post.

Class President Mia Alvaros with Principal Todd

Each homeroom elected a candidate to run for president. Four names, one from each homeroom, went on the final ballot: Ethan Knox, Mia Alvaros, Olivia Snow, and Zayden Jackson.

On Monday, each class member had a chance to vote for their choice. It was a close race, but the final tally showed a clear winner.

Mia Alvaros has been a student here since kindergarten. She has participated in many school activities, including track, choir, and book club. Alvaros promised to work for all students and to make this the best year ever

Unusual details will hold your readers' attention.

CHAPTER SIX

Your Own Byline

Reporters put their names under the headline. This is called a **byline**. Anyone reading the story will know who wrote it.

Maybe someday you will be a news reporter for a big newspaper. Then we will read stories with your byline!

Ask your friends and family to offer comments on your articles.

ACTIVITY

Did I Choose a Newsworthy Topic?

Read your news article. Carefully check everything one more time. Ask yourself these questions:

- Did I answer the questions: who, what, where, when, why, and how?
- Did I begin my news article with a lead?
- Did I include facts in the body?
- Did I end the article with a conclusion?
- Did I include a catchy headline?
- Did I include an illustration with a caption?
- Did I use my byline?
- Did I use correct spelling and grammar?

GLOSSARY

articles (AHR-tih-kuhlz) pieces of writing published in newspapers, magazines, or online

body (BAH-dee) the main text of an article

byline (BYE-line) a line at the beginning of an article that gives the author's name

caption (KAP-shuhn) a short description that appears with an illustration

conclusion (kuhn-KLOO-zhuhn) the end of something

current (KUR-uhnt) happening now

engaging (en-GAY-jing) interesting or entertaining

headline (HED-line) the title of an article in a newspaper, magazine, or website

illustrate (IL-uh-strayt) add or include pictures

lead (LEED) the first sentence of a news article

platform (PLAT-form) a statement of beliefs

reporters (rih-POR-turz) people who gather and report the news

sources (SORS-ez) people who provide information or materials found in libraries or online

verify (VER-uh-fye) to confirm that a fact is true

For More INFORMATION

BOOKS

Cupp, Dave, and Cecilia Minden. *TV-Station Secrets*. Mankato, MN: The Child's World, 2009.

Flora, Sherrill B., and Jo Browning-Wroe. *The Fairy Tale Times: 10 Fairy Tales Rewritten as High-Interest Front Page News Articles*. Minneapolis, MN: Key Education Publishing, 2006.

WEBSITES

ReadWriteThink Printing Press
http://www.readwritethink.org/classroom-resources/student-interactives/printing-press-30036.html
Use this website to create your own newspaper.

Time for Kids
www.timeforkids.com
Read news articles about many interesting topics at this *Time* magazine site.

INDEX

body, 10
byline, 20

caption, 16
conclusion, 10
current events, 6

details, 4, 19

facts, 4, 8–9

headlines, 16–17

lead, 10
listening, 6

news article
   headline, 16–17
   organizing, 10–13
   sample, 18
   verifying, 8
   what it is, 4–7
   writing, 14–15

opening sentence, 10
outline, 11

picture, 16

questions, 8

reporters, 4, 6, 8, 14, 20
research, 8

About the AUTHORS

Cecilia Minden is the former director of the Language and Literacy Program at Harvard Graduate School of Education. She earned her doctorate from the University of Virginia. Her research focused on early literacy skills. She is currently a literacy consultant and the author of over 100 books for children. Dr. Minden lives with her family in McKinney, Texas. She loves to spend time reading books and writing to family and friends.

Kate Roth has a doctorate from Harvard University in language and literacy and a master's degree from Columbia University Teachers College in curriculum and teaching. Her work focuses on writing instruction in the primary grades. She has taught kindergarten, first grade, and Reading Recovery. She has also instructed hundreds of teachers from around the world in early literacy practices. She lived with her husband and three children in China for many years, and now they live in Connecticut.